D1299804

JAN   2012

Grow It Yourself!

Grow Your Own
SOUP

John Malam

Heinemann Library
Chicago, Illinois

www.heinemannraintree.com
Visit our website to find out more information about Heinemann-Raintree books.

To order:
☎ Phone 888-454-2279
💻 Visit www.heinemannraintree.com to browse our catalog and order online.

© 2012 Heinemann Library
an imprint of Capstone Global Library, LLC
Chicago, Illinois

Edited by Daniel Nunn, Rebecca Rissman, and Sian Smith
Designed by Philippa Jenkins
Picture research by Mica Brancic
Originated by Capstone Global Library Ltd
Printed and bound in China by Leo Paper Products Ltd

15 14 13 12 11
10 9 8 7 6 5 4 3 2 1

Library of Congress Cataloging-in-Publication Data
Malam, John, 1957-
  Grow your own soup / John Malam.—1st ed.
      p. cm.—(Grow it yourself!)
  Includes bibliographical references and index.
  ISBN 978-1-4329-5106-1 (hc)—ISBN 978-1-4329-5113-9
(pb) 1. Pumpkin—Planting—Juvenile literature. 2. Pumpkin—
Seeds—Juvenile literature. 3. Cooking (Pumpkin)—Juvenile
literature. I. Title.
  SB347.M35 2012
  635'.62—dc22   2010049830

Acknowledgments
The author and publisher are grateful to the following for permission to reproduce copyright material: Alamy p. 18 (© Alison Thompson); © Capstone Publishers pp. 13, 15, 21, 26, 27, 28, 29 bottom, 29 top (Karon Dubke); Corbis p. 6 (© Robert Galbraith/Reuters); GAP Photos pp. 9 (Christine Bollen), 11 (Maxine Adcock), 20 (Zara Napier); iStockphoto p. 23 (© Rich Legg); © John Malam pp. 24, 25; Photolibrary pp. 4 (Garden Picture Library/Stephen Shepherd), 8 (Garden Picture Library/Mark Bolton), 14 (Garden Picture Library/ Francesca Yorke); Shutterstock pp. 5 (© Marilyn Volan), 7 (© Stephen Coburn), 10, 17, 19 (© Denis and Yulia Pogostins), 12 (© Losevsky Pavel), 16 (© Saiko3p), 22 (© Tatagatta).

Background cover photograph of pumpkins in a Thanksgiving fair reproduced with permission of Shutterstock (© Ckchiu). Foreground cover photograph of a bowl of pumpkin soup reproduced with permission of © Capstone Publishers (Karon Dubke)

To find out about the author, visit his website: www.johnmalam.co.uk

Every effort has been made to contact copyright holders of any material reproduced in this book. Any omissions will be rectified in subsequent printings if notice is given to the publisher.

All the Internet addresses (URLs) given in this book were valid at the time of going to press. However, due to the dynamic nature of the Internet, some addresses may have changed, or sites may have changed or ceased to exist since publication. While the author and publisher regret any inconvenience this may cause readers, no responsibility for any such changes can be accepted by either the author or the publisher.

Some words are shown in bold, **like this**. You can find out what they mean by looking in the glossary.

Contents

Safety note:
Ask an adult to help you with
the activities in this book.

What is a Pumpkin?

A pumpkin is the **fruit** of the pumpkin plant. It is usually orange, but it can also be red, yellow, or white. Inside is the flesh and the **seeds**.

A big, round pumpkin is heavy! ▶

Farmers grow long rows of pumpkins in fields.

A few weeks after pumpkin **seeds** have been **sown**, the plants make flowers. After a few days, baby pumpkins appear. When they are **ripe**, they are ready to pick. Pumpkins are a healthy food.

Big and Small

There are many types of pumpkins. Some are mini pumpkins, the size of oranges. Other pumpkins become giant. The biggest pumpkins are the heaviest fruits in the world.

There are competitions to grow giant pumpkins, like these.

Some pumpkins are small.

Each type of pumpkin has a name. Jack-Be-Little is the name of a mini pumpkin. Atlantic Giant is the name of a monster-sized pumpkin. Pumpkin names can be funny, such as Red Warty Thing!

Creepers and Climbers

Pumpkin plants grow by creeping along the ground, or by climbing up frames. Big pumpkins grow on creeping plants because of their size and weight.

Pumpkin plants spread or creep across the ground before they make their fruit.

mini pumpkin

frame

Mini pumpkins are much smaller and lighter than their bigger cousins. Mini pumpkins can be grown to climb up frames.

Where to Grow

Pumpkin plants are grown outside on open ground. They grow into very big plants. They need a lot of space to spread out, especially if they are the type that creep along the ground.

This pumpkin plant is gradually creeping across the soil.

Pumpkins will grow over the sides of large pots like this.

The plants like to grow in a sunny spot in a border or a vegetable patch. They can also be grown in large pots or **planters**—but they still need a lot of space to spread out.

Get Ready to Grow!

Plant nurseries have everything you need for growing pumpkin plants. Some stores and supermarkets also sell the same equipment.

There are many different types of pumpkin seeds to choose from.

To grow your own pumpkin plants you will need a pack of pumpkin **seeds**. Choose a creeping type that produces good-sized orange **fruit**, such as Howden.

You will also need: seed **compost**, medium plant pots (about 5 inches wide), labels, liquid plant food, and a watering can with a sprinkler head.

Sowing the Seeds

1. In April, fill the plant pots with **seed compost**.
2. Gently push the pumpkin seeds about 2 inches into the compost. **Sow** one seed in each pot.

Pumpkin seeds are big and easy to hold.

3. Push the seeds in edge first, not flat. This is to stop them from **rotting** if they are given too much water.

4. Sprinkle on enough compost to cover the seeds, and then label the pots.

5. Water the pots, then put them in a warm place inside. Don't let the compost dry out!

Successful Seedlings

For the pumpkin **seeds** to grow, they need warmth and water. Keep the **compost moist**, but do not overwater it or the seeds will **rot** away. After about fourteen days, the pumpkin plants will start to appear.

The first two leaves are called "**seed leaves**."

The first true leaf has grown.

true leaf

seed leaves

At first, the plants have two seed leaves. These are soon followed by **true leaves**. The **seedlings** will grow fast, pushing up through the compost and making lots of large leaves. Keep watering them.

17

Planting Out

By June, the plants will start growing bigger. Get them used to living outside. Put them outside in the day, then bring them inside at night.

baby pumpkin plant

Dig a hole for the pumpkin plant. Put **compost** in the bottom of the hole to feed the plant.

Remove the plants from their pots. Put them into holes in the ground.

After a few days they will be ready to **plant out** into the ground. You will only need to plant one or two. Water them after planting.

Watering and Feeding

Ask an adult to cut the bottom off a large plastic bottle. Then push the neck into the soil near the plant. When you pour water into it, it will go deep into the soil near the **roots**.

Pumpkin plants need a lot of water.

Instructions on the liquid plant feed will tell you how much to use.

Pumpkin plants are hungry. Once a week, give them a feed. Mix a liquid plant food into their water. It contains all the **nutrients** they will need.

Don't Forget the Weeding!

Weeds can be a problem, especially while the pumpkin plants are young and still quite small. Weeds take water in the soil away from the pumpkin plants.

Remove as many weeds as you can.

Pumpkin plants will grow well in this weed-free patch.

Pull weeds out, or dig them up with a **hand trowel** or **hand fork**. You could cut through them with a **garden hoe**. Be careful not to damage the pumpkin plants.

23

From Flower to Fruit

In July, large yellow flowers appear. Some are at the end of long, thin stalks. These are male flowers. Some have short stalks and a swollen part at the end, near the **stem**. These are female flowers.

swelling

short stalk

female flower

The swelling at the end of this female flower is the start of a pumpkin.

By September or October the pumpkin will be large. ▶

green skin changes to orange

The flowers make **pollen** that bees take from flower to flower. Baby pumpkins appear at the ends of the female flowers and begin to grow. Soon the pumpkins change color from green to orange and are ready to pick.

Make Pumpkin Soup

Ask an adult to help you with the cutting and cooking.
You will need:
1 large pumpkin, 2 large onions, 4 cloves of garlic, water, milk, salt, and pepper.

1. Cut the pumpkin in half.
2. Remove the **seeds** and stringy parts.
   Peel the skin off.

3. Cut the pumpkin into small chunks.
4. Peel and chop the onions and garlic.
5. Put the pumpkin chunks, onion, and garlic into a large pan. Add water until they are almost covered.
6. Bring to the boil, then cook gently until the pumpkin is soft.

7. Remove the pan from the heat and leave it to cool.

8. Use a hand blender to blend everything together until it is smooth. It will be quite thick.

Roasted pumpkin seeds

Pumpkin **seeds** also make a tasty snack. Wash the seeds and spread them out on a cookie sheet. Place in a hot oven for about 30 minutes. Sprinkle with salt, then serve.

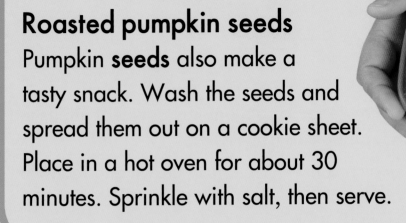

9. To serve, return to the heat and stir in some milk, or milk and water. This will thin the soup down. Add salt and pepper to taste.

Glossary

compost loose, earthy material used for growing seeds and plants

fruit part of a plant which can often be eaten as food. Fruit contains seeds.

garden hoe gardening tool with a flat blade and a long wooden handle

hand fork small gardening tool with three pointed prongs

hand trowel gardening tool similar to a small spade with a curved edge

moist when soil is damp but not too wet

nutrients substances that help to keep plants healthy

plant out when a plant is put into its final growing place

planter large container used for growing a plant in

pollen tiny powdery grains made by flowers

ripe fully grown and ready to pick or eat

root part of a plant that holds it in the ground. Roots collect water for the plant.

rot when a plant starts to go bad

seed part of a plant that grows into a new plant

seed leaves first two simple leaves of a plant

seedling baby plant

sow to plant a seed

sown to have planted a seed

stem main branch or trunk of a plant

true leaves all the leaves that come after the seed leaves

Find Out More

Books to read

Grow It, Eat It. New York: Dorling Kindersley, 2008.

Websites

www.backyardgardener.com/pumpkin.html
Look at photos of record-breaking giant pumpkins on this Website and find out more about them.

www.kiddiegardens.com
This Website will give you lots of ideas on how to grow plants to eat.

www.kiddiegardens.com/growing_pumpkins.html
This Website is packed with advice and tips on how to grow pumpkins.

Index